SECRETS OF
ANIMAL
LIFE CYCLES

ANDREW SOLWAY

 **Marshall Cavendish**
Benchmark
New York

This edition first published in 2011 in the United States of America
by MARSHALL CAVENDISH BENCHMARK
An imprint of Marshall Cavendish Corporation

This publication represents the opinions and views of the author based on Andrew Solway's personal experience, knowledge, and research. The information in this book serves as a general guide only. The author and publisher have used their best efforts in preparing this book and disclaim liability rising directly and indirectly from the use and application of this book.

Planned and produced by Discovery Books Ltd., 2 College Street, Ludlow, Shropshire, SY8 1AN www.discoverybooks.net
Managing editor: Paul Humphrey
Editor: Clare Hibbert
Designer: sprout.uk.com Limited
Illustrator: Stefan Chabluk
Picture researcher: Tom Humphrey

Photo acknowledgments: Alamy: p 11 (Bob Gibbons); Corbis: pp 15 (W. Wayne Lockwood, M.D.), 23 (MedicalRF.com), 25 (DLILLC), 27 (Jean Francois Istel/Sygma); FLPA: pp 20 (Suzi Eszterhas/Minden Pictures), 22 (Nigel Cattlin); Getty Images: pp 10 (Paul Zahl/National Geographic), 12 (Bianca Lavies/National Geographic), 13 (Nicole Duplaix), 19 (Image Source), 28 (Adrian Bailey); IStockphoto: p 5 (Eduardo Jose Bernardino); NHPA: pp 8 (Rich Kirchner), 26 (Stephen Dalton); Shutterstock Images: cover eggs (Vishnevskiy Vasily), cover bee (Seleznev Valery), cover and pp 1 chicks (Cheryl E. Davis), 14 (Nickolay Stanev), 16 (Dr Morley Read); Wikimedia: pp 7 (Yotcmdr), 24 (Mehmet Karatay).

Other Marshall Cavendish Offices:
Marshall Cavendish International (Asia) Private Limited, 1 New Industrial Road, Singapore 536196 • Marshall Cavendish International (Thailand) Co Ltd. 253 Asoke, 12th Flr, Sukhumvit 21 Road, Klongtoey Nua, Wattana, Bangkok 10110, Thailand • Marshall Cavendish (Malaysia) Sdn Bhd, Times Subang, Lot 46, Subang Hi-Tech Industrial Park, Batu Tiga, 40000 Shah Alam, Selangor Darul Ehsan, Malaysia

Marshall Cavendish is a trademark of Times Publishing Limited

The website addresses (URLs) included in this book were valid at the time of going to press. However, because of the nature of the Internet, it is possible that some addresses may have changed, or the sites may have changed or closed down since publication. While the author, packager, and the publisher regret any inconvenience this may cause to the readers, no responsibility for any such changes can be accepted by the author, packager, or publisher.

Every attempt has been made to clear copyright. Should there be any inadvertent omission, please apply to the publisher for rectification.

Library of Congress Cataloging-in-Publication Data

Solway, Andrew.
  Secrets of animal life cycles / Andrew Solway.
     p. cm. -- (Science secrets)
  Includes index.
  ISBN 978-1-60870-135-3
1. Animal life cycles--Juvenile literature. I. Title.
  QL49.S669 2011
  591.56--dc22
                       2009050538

Printed in China
1 3 6 5 4 2

Contents

What's In a Life Cycle?

Do your parents have pictures of you when you were a baby? If they do, how do you look? You probably look very different from the way you look now! You have changed a lot since you were born, and you will change in other ways as you grow and get older.

Life Changes

All animals change over time. They are born from their mother or hatch from an egg, they grow and become adults, then they get old and die. This is a life cycle.

When animals become adults, they are able to **reproduce** (produce young).

When the **offspring** (young) are born, they begin a new life cycle.

▼ *The human life cycle. Children are born and grow into adults, who reproduce and have more children.*

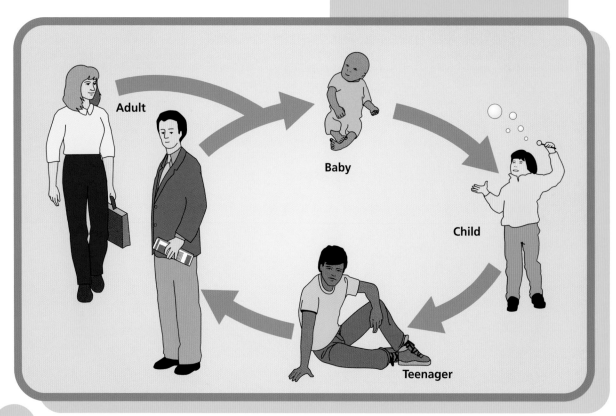

Adult

Baby

Child

Teenager

Learning About Life Cycles

In this book, you will find out more about animal life cycles. As you read, you will learn secrets about how different animals are born, grow, reproduce, and die.

Why do some animals change completely as they grow up? Why are eggs so amazing? And what happens to animals when they die?

▼ This little girl, her mother, and her grandmother are all at different stages of the human life cycle.

FAMILY CHANGES

Look for photos of yourself when you were a baby. How different do you look? Would you recognize yourself if no one had told you who was in the photo?

See if you can find pictures of your parents and other family members when they were young. Can you recognize them? Why or why not?

How Long Does a Life Cycle Last?

Some insects live only for a week. Mice live for just a few years. Humans, whales, and tortoises, however, can live for more than one hundred years.

Live Fast, Die Young

Animals that have short lives must cram everything into a short amount of time. Mice are adults at around six weeks old, and they produce their first young only three weeks later.

Other animals have even shorter lives. The pygmy goby, a small fish, lives an average of only fifty-nine days. Mayflies and some kinds of midge spend less than a day as adults.

▼ *The maximum life spans of some different animals (some were in zoos).*

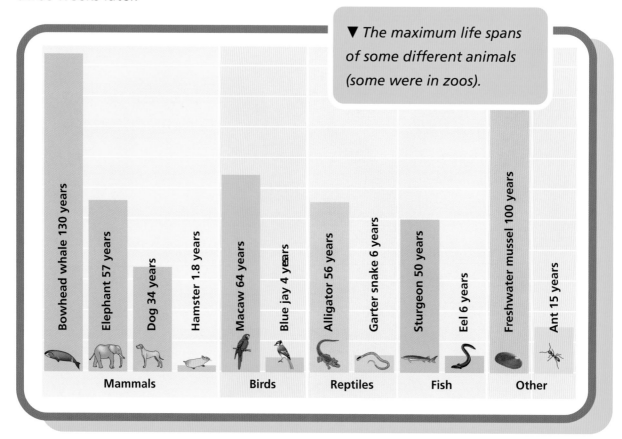

Bowhead whale 130 years
Elephant 57 years
Dog 34 years
Hamster 1.8 years
Mammals

Macaw 64 years
Blue jay 4 years
Birds

Alligator 56 years
Garter snake 6 years
Reptiles

Sturgeon 50 years
Eel 6 years
Fish

Freshwater mussel 100 years
Ant 15 years
Other

Slow and Steady

Humans are among the longest-lived animals. However, we are not the record breakers. Giant tortoises can live for more than 170 years. They do not become adults until they are 20 or 25. Bowhead whales have been found with **harpoon** heads that are over 100 years old stuck in their skin. Parrots and albatrosses are among the longest-lived birds. Albatrosses do not begin to reproduce until they are ten years old.

▲ *Giant tortoises, such as this one from the Seychelles Islands, can live for more than 170 years.*

SCIENCE SECRETS

LONG LIVES

Scientists have discovered ocean animals that live far longer than giant tortoises. A clam caught off the coast of Iceland was found to be 405 years old. Even more amazing, there is a kind of **sponge** in the Antarctic that can live for more than 1,500 years.

How Many Animals Lay Eggs?

Eighty percent of all animals hatch from eggs. These eggs can be as different from each other as the animals that produce them.

Eggs of All Kinds

Many fish eggs are no bigger than the head of a pin, while an ostrich egg is the size of a small melon. Insect eggs have a tough outer case, while frog and toad eggs have a thick coating of jelly. Many **reptile** eggs have a leathery shell, while bird eggshells are hard and brittle.

Life-support System

An egg is an amazing life-support system. A bird's egg has a strong outer shell that lets air in and out but not water. The shell's rounded shape evenly

▼ *Fish such as these salmon gather at special **breeding grounds** to spawn (lay eggs and reproduce).*

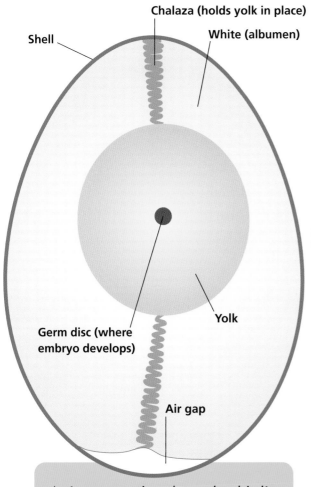

Shell

Chalaza (holds yolk in place)

White (albumen)

Yolk

Germ disc (where embryo develops)

Air gap

▲ *A cross-section through a bird's egg, showing the structure. The two chalazae hold the egg yolk in the middle of the egg.*

spreads any pressure on it, so it does not crack when the parents sit on it. At the same time, the shell is fragile enough to be broken open by the baby bird inside when it is ready to hatch. The yolk provides a rich source of food, while the albumen (white) provides water and also helps cushion and protect the **embryo**.

EXPERIMENT

TESTING EGG STRENGTH

This experiment allows you to test how strong a chicken's egg is.

You will need:
- an egg carton containing six eggs
- a piece of plastic food wrap • lots of paperback books (ask permission if you are borrowing these) • bathroom scales

1. Remove the top from the egg carton. Make sure that the tops of the eggs are all level in the carton. Put plastic food wrap on top of them to protect the books if the eggs break.

2. One at a time, place the paperbacks on top of the eggs. See how many books you can balance before the eggs crack.

3. Use a bathroom scale to weigh the books you used, so you know how much weight the eggs were able to support—it could be more than 8.8 pounds (4 kg)!

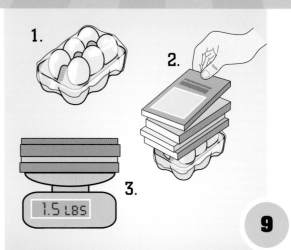

1.

2.

3.

1.5 LBS

Do All Animals Take Care of Their Eggs?

At least some of an animal's eggs must survive to become adults. If they do not, the whole **species** will eventually die out. Many animals ensure that some of their young will survive to adulthood by producing huge numbers of eggs.

Cod Survival

A female cod can produce 100 million eggs in her lifetime. She releases them into the water and leaves them to survive as best they can. Millions are eaten or damaged before they hatch, and millions more die young. Only about one egg in 10 million becomes an adult. So, of those 100 million eggs, a female cod only produces ten cod that live to become adults.

Less Is More

Some animals produce fewer eggs, but care for them to make sure that as many as possible reach adulthood.

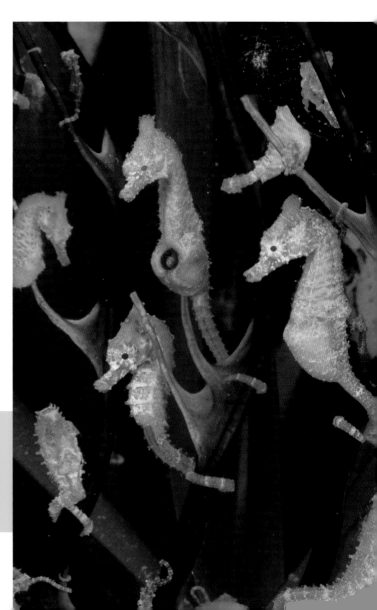

▶ These male seahorses are *"pregnant."* Females lay their eggs in a pouch on the male's belly and he carries them until they hatch.

Wolf spiders carry their eggs in a large **sac** until they hatch. Some species of spider even carry the hatched spiderlings around on their back. Male sticklebacks (a kind of **freshwater** fish) make a "nest" for the eggs and protect them until they hatch. Other fish carry their eggs in their mouth. The female marsupial tree frog carries her eggs around in a pouch on her back. Most birds sit on their eggs to help them hatch, and then feed the young after hatching.

EXPERIMENT

EGG HUNT

Go on an egg-hunting expedition in your yard or a local park.

Look under leaves and on plant stems for insect eggs. Sometimes these may be protected—"cuckoo spit" (blobs of white froth found on many plants) is a protective coating around batches of **froghopper** eggs.

1. Look in small ponds for frog or toad spawn (eggs).

2. You are unlikely to find bird's eggs, but be sure not to touch them or to stay too long nearby if you do, or the parents may abandon the eggs.

3. Record what you find by drawing or photographing the eggs. Return after a few days. Are the eggs still there? Can you find any new ones?

◄ *"Cuckoo spit" has nothing to do with cuckoos. It is made by insects called froghoppers to protect their eggs.*

Which Animals Give Birth?

Not all animals lay eggs. Some give birth to live young. **Mammals** such as humans, dogs, and cats produce young in this way, but so do other animals. Some snakes and lizards, many sharks, and even some insects also give birth.

Advantages of Live Young

When animals are born live, the embryos develop inside their mother's body instead of in an egg. The growing embryos are well protected, and they get food, water, and air from their mother.

It is easier to keep developing embryos warm inside the mother's body than in an egg. So animals such as reptiles, which normally lay eggs, sometimes produce live young when they live in cold conditions.

On the Move

A mother that produces live young has no eggs to guard or to keep warm. Her developing babies are safe inside her, so she is free to go off in search of food. This is a big advantage for animals that are always on the move.

▼ *A garter snake giving birth. Garter snakes live in cold climates, so they produce live young instead of eggs.*

UNUSUAL MAMMALS

Nearly all mammals produce live young. However, four species lay eggs—the platypus and three kinds of echidna (spiny anteater). They are known as monotremes.

When a reptile or bird lays an egg, the embryo inside is just a tiny dot. It has a lot of growing to do before it hatches. When a monotreme lays an egg, the young animal inside has already done lots of growing and is almost ready to hatch.

Kangaroos belong to another group of mammals called **marsupials**. Marsupial young are very tiny and helpless when they are born. They crawl over their mother's body to a pouch on her belly. They develop inside the pouch, feeding on their mother's milk.

▲ *Platypuses are one of the few kinds of mammal that lay eggs. They live in and around rivers in eastern Australia*

Do All Offspring Need Their Parents?

Some newborns cannot survive without their parents. Ants and bees, chicks, kittens, and wolf cubs, for example, are all helpless when they are very young. They rely on their parents, or other adults, for food and protection.

Lots to Learn

Many birds and mammals need their parents for more than food and shelter. They have to be taught skills to help them survive. Lion cubs learn how to hunt from their mothers. Orangutans have to learn a "map" of the rain forest, so that they can find food at all times of year. Male songbirds learn complex songs from listening to their parents and other adult birds.

Natural Know-how

Not all young animals are fed and protected. Most of them have to care for themselves. They do not need to learn the skills they need for survival. They are born with this knowledge. Garden spiders, for example, know

▼ This zebra foal can run within minutes of birth. However, it will need its mother's milk and protection for more than a year.

SCIENCE SECRETS

SHARED CHILDCARE

Some young animals are looked after by other adults, as well as their parents. Anis are tropical cuckoos. When they are ready to breed, a group of anis build a nest together, and several females lay their eggs in it. The whole group then shares the task of hatching the eggs and feeding the chicks.

Some mammals also share caring for their young. Female elephants in a herd often have their young at about the same time. They then share the work of feeding and caring for them.

how to build a web without any tips from their parents. Crocodiles and tiger sharks are born with a full set of teeth, ready to start hunting.

▼ *The great challenge for young birds is learning to fly. These blue heron fledglings are exercising their wings before trying to fly.*

Why Do Some Animals Change as They Grow?

Some baby animals do not look anything like the adults of their species. The best-known examples are caterpillars, which turn into elegant butterflies, and tadpoles, which become frogs. The transformation these animals make is known as **metamorphosis**.

Metamorphosis

Ants, bees, beetles, butterflies, flies, and wasps change completely as they grow. This is called complete metamorphosis. The young that hatch from the eggs are known as **larvae**. Insect larvae are eating machines. They have powerful jaws for chopping up their food.

Once a larva reaches a certain size, it changes to become a **pupa**. A pupa is protected by a cocoon, or outer covering, and stays in one place. Inside, the larva's body breaks down completely and re-forms itself. Then the pupa splits open and the adult insect crawls out.

▼ *This young frog still has the remains of its tadpole tail, but it also has four strong legs.*

HIDING FROM ENEMIES

Caterpillars (butterfly larvae) make a tempting snack for a bird or other animal. To protect themselves, many are **camouflaged** to look like their surroundings. Some match the leaves they feed on; others look like dead leaves or flower parts.

Swallowtail caterpillars have two kinds of defense. When they are small, they disguise themselves to look like bird droppings. Later, they develop poisons inside their body that make them taste horrible so that **predators** spit them out.

Why Change?

Metamorphosis allows an animal to specialize at different stages of its life. Insect larvae concentrate on eating and growing. They stay in a small area. Adult insects usually have wings—they are built to travel and reproduce. Specializing has helped insects to spread to every part of the planet.

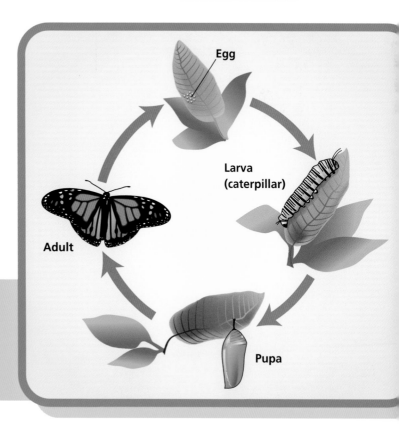

Egg

Larva (caterpillar)

Adult

Pupa

▶ *The metamorphosis of a monarch butterfly, from egg to larva (caterpillar) to pupa (cocoon) to adult.*

Do All Insects Metamorphose?

Not all insects go through the life cycle from egg to larva to pupa to adult. Insects such as dragonflies, mayflies, and grasshoppers change gradually as they grow. This kind of change is called partial metamorphosis.

Molting

All insects have a tough outer "skin," called an exoskeleton. This gives them protection, but it does not grow like the rest of the body. As an insect grows, it has to **molt** (shed its exoskeleton) from time to time.

Growing Bigger

In insects that change through partial metamorphosis, the body changes with each molt. In grasshoppers, these changes are only slight. They get bigger with each molt, and on their final molt they develop wings.

Bigger Changes

In some insects, including dragonflies and damselflies, the changes are bigger. A dragonfly **nymph** (young dragonfly) lives underwater, at the bottom of a pool or pond. For its final molt, it crawls up a plant stem and out of the water. When its skin splits, a winged adult dragonfly crawls out.

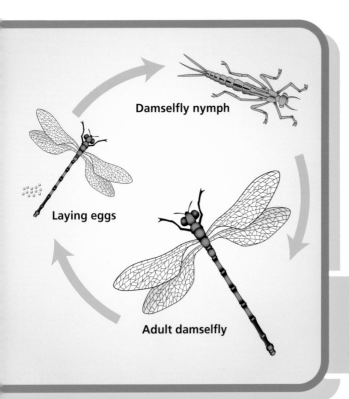

Damselfly nymph

Laying eggs

Adult damselfly

◀ *Damselfly nymphs live underwater for one or two years, but the adult insects live for only a few weeks.*

POND DIPPING

Try pond dipping to find insect nymphs and larvae. For safety, make sure you go with an adult.

You will need:
• a net or kitchen sieve • a tray or other shallow container (preferably white) • a strainer and spoon to scoop out creatures • a smaller container for individual creatures • a magnifying glass

1. Put some pond water in your tray.

2. Sweep your net or sieve back and forth in the pond, then tip its contents into your tray. What have you netted?

3. Try dipping at different levels in the pond. Did you find different creatures?

4. Use the pictures on this page and information from reference books and the Internet to identify some of the creatures you discover.

5. When you have finished, put your finds back in the pond at the place where you found them.

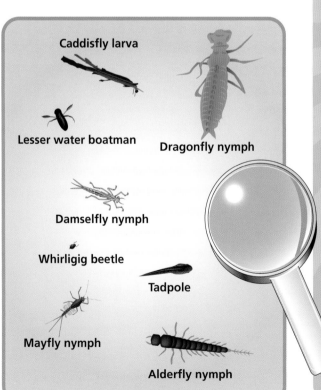

Caddisfly larva

Lesser water boatman

Dragonfly nymph

Damselfly nymph

Whirligig beetle

Tadpole

Mayfly nymph

Alderfly nymph

Why Do Animals Migrate?

Some animals spend part of the year in one place and the rest of the year somewhere else many miles away. This yearly round trip is called **migration**. It is an important part of the life cycle of many animals. But why do animals migrate?

Traveling to Breed

Many animals migrate to **breed**. Some frogs and toads, for example, live on land as adults, but they must lay their eggs in water. Every spring, frogs migrate back to the lakes and ponds where they were born, so the females can lay their eggs.

Sea turtles live in water but must lay their eggs on land. They migrate the other way, traveling across thousands of miles of ocean to lay their eggs on breeding beaches.

▼ *Every year, nearly 1.5 million wildebeest migrate in a circle around the African savannah in search of fresh grass.*

CHAMPION FLYERS

In 2006, scientists discovered that the sooty shearwater was a champion of long-distance migration. Researchers fitted the seabirds with electronic tags and tracked them across the Pacific. They found that the birds traveled over 40,000 miles (64,000 km) every year, from New Zealand to Japan, Russia, or Alaska and back. Arctic terns, which travel from the North to the South Pole each year, may fly even farther, but they are too small to tag.

Traveling to Eat

Other animals migrate to find food. In the grasslands of southern Africa, the grass withers and dies in the **dry season**, then new growth comes in the **rainy season**. The rainy season happens at different times in different places, so antelope, wildebeest, and other grazing animals migrate to find new grass.

▶ *The migration routes of the sooty shearwater and the Arctic tern are probably the longest in the world.*

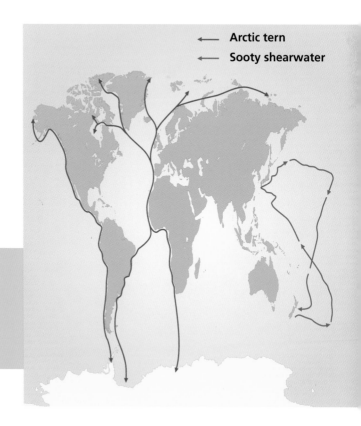

← Arctic tern
← Sooty shearwater

How Does a New Life Begin?

We think of a new life beginning when a baby is born or an egg hatches. But the young animal spends weeks or months growing before it is born. So how exactly does life begin?

Egg Cells

All animals produce special **cells** for reproduction. Females produce egg cells, while males produce sperm cells.

An egg cell is not the same as an egg. It is a tiny "bag" of chemicals that contains the ingredients for a new animal. When an egg cell begins to grow, it divides in two. This is the point at which a new life begins.

Males and Females

Some simple living things can reproduce just by dividing in two. Some female animals can lay eggs that then develop without the help of a male. Both these ways of reproducing are called **asexual reproduction**.

▼ Female aphids can reproduce asexually. They lay eggs that can grow without being fertilized. The offspring are **clones** of their mother.

However, most animals need males and females to reproduce. This is known as **sexual reproduction**. In animals that reproduce sexually, an egg cell cannot begin to grow until it has combined with a sperm cell. When an egg cell and a sperm cell are joined, the egg cell is **fertilized**. It starts to divide and grow.

The fertilized egg will become a completely new animal, inheriting some characteristics from its mother and some from its father.

▲ *This ball of cells is a fertilized human egg after it has divided just a few times.*

THE "INSTRUCTION BOOK" OF LIFE

The secret of sexual reproduction is a special material found in the nucleus (center) of a cell. This **genetic material**, or DNA, carries all the information the cell needs to grow into a new living thing.

How Do Animals Find Mates?

Reproduction is a vital part of the life cycle. If animals cannot reproduce, they die out. So it is important for adult animals to find the right **mate** (partner).

Fights and Displays

In many animal species, the female chooses her mate. The males compete with each other to attract the female's attention. They have different ways of doing this. Many male birds put on fantastic displays to get attention, even performing acrobatics in midair. Crickets, bullfrogs, and songbirds "sing" to attract a female.

▼ *Red deer stags (males) grow large antlers each year. They sometimes clash antlers in competition for mates.*

▲ *Red-crowned cranes usually pair for life. They dance together, bowing and stretching, when choosing a mate.*

Often, males fight each other to show who is strongest. Some animals have "weapons" that they use to fight, such as a male deer's antlers. Usually the fights are not too serious and neither animal is badly hurt.

Smells and Dances

In some cases, the females attract the males. Female moths produce a special scent that can attract males from as far away as 6 miles (10 km). In other species, males and females both display; for example, some birds perform elaborate courtship dances.

DEADLY FLASHES

Female fireflies sit on the ground and produce flashes of light to attract flying males. Each kind of firefly has its own special flashing pattern. However, the females of one firefly (*Photuris*) mimic the flashing pattern of another species. When the males fly down to investigate, the *Photuris* female eats them!

How Do Animals Die?

Dying is the final stage in the life cycle. Very few animals die of old age. Most do not even survive to become adults. So how do most animals die?

Killed by Predators

The majority of animals that die young are killed by predators (animals that eat other animals). For example, birds eat huge numbers of insects and spiders, while big cats such as lions and cheetahs are the main predators of antelope and other African grassland grazers.

Lions, sharks, and other top predators are often killed by their own kind. For example, if a male lion takes over a pride (lion group), he may kill the old pride leader. He will also kill any young cubs that he did not father.

▼ *With one flash of its long, sticky tongue, a chameleon ends the life cycle of an insect on a flower.*

► *Human activity, including pollution, causes many animals to die. This bird has been killed by oil spilled from a tanker.*

Starving to Death

Lack of food is another big killer. In a harsh winter, animals may not be able to find enough food to survive. Sometimes, the whole population of one kind of animal is affected. For example, in some years the number of **lemmings** drops dramatically because of food shortages. This is also disastrous for animals that eat lemmings, such as snowy owls.

SCIENCE SECRETS

DYING TO BREED

Some animals breed only once and then die. Pacific salmon are a good example. Each year, millions of adult salmon swim from the ocean to breeding grounds in freshwater streams. After breeding, the salmon lie exhausted and die in the water. Bald eagles, bears, and other **scavengers** gather in large numbers to feast on them.

What Happens to an Animal After It Dies?

The death of an animal is not the end of the life story. If an animal is eaten by a predator, its body provides food to keep that predator alive.

Leftovers

After the predator has eaten its fill, scavengers, such as vultures and hyenas, feed on the leftovers. The last little scraps are a meal for maggots (fly larvae), beetles, and worms. Anything left by the maggots is **decomposed** (broken down) by **bacteria** and **fungi** to become part of the soil.

The Life Spiral

If an animal reproduces before it dies, it leaves more than its body behind. Each of its offspring starts a new life cycle, growing and developing, reproducing, and dying. The life cycle of one animal begins and ends, but each is part of a life spiral that goes on and on.

▼ *This dead minke whale is a feast for hundreds of ghost crabs.*

ROTTEN MELON

See decomposers in action.

You will need:
• two small chunks of melon • two jars with holes in the lids (ask an adult to make the holes) • some soil

Put some damp soil in one jar, and leave the other empty. Add a small chunk of melon to each jar and screw on the lids.

Look at the jars every two days for two weeks. Write down any changes (you could take photos). Take the lid off and sniff: Is there a smell? How quickly do the melon chunks change? Do both chunks change in the same way?

Both melon chunks will slowly change because of chemical reactions inside and on the surface. However, decomposers living in the soil speed up the process of the melon breaking down.

▼ *The cycle of life is more like a spiral. It does not go back to the same beginning. In each generation, new animals are born.*

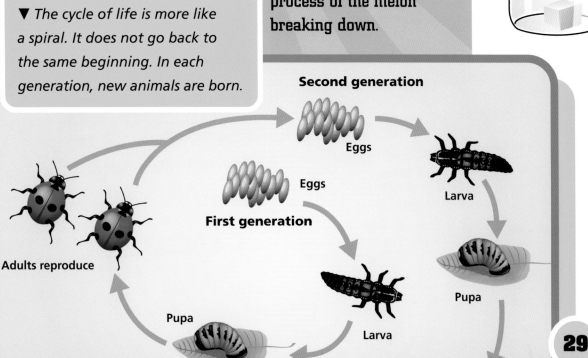

Second generation

Eggs

Eggs

First generation

Larva

Larva

Pupa

Pupa

Adults reproduce

Pupa

Glossary

asexual reproduction When a living thing reproduces without a mate by dividing, or by splitting off a part of itself to produce offspring that are identical to itself.

bacterium (plural bacteria) A very tiny, simple type of living thing that has just a single cell.

breed To reproduce (produce offspring).

breeding ground Place where animals gather to breed.

camouflage To be colored and shaped so as to blend in with the surrounding environment.

cell One of the billions of tiny living parts that make up every animal or plant. A cell is the smallest unit of life.

clone A living thing that is an exact copy of its parent, sharing the same DNA.

cocoon A pupa in a tube-shaped, protective outer casing made from sticky silk thread.

decomposed Rotted, or broken down, into smaller parts or simple chemicals.

dry season One of the two seasons that occur in tropical parts of the world (the other is the rainy season).

embryo The very early stage of a developing animal, before it is born or has hatched from an egg.

fertilized Able to develop into a new living thing, for example an egg cell that has joined with a sperm cell.

froghopper A kind of small, brown insect that can jump long distances. Its large wings are folded like a tent across its back.

fungus (plural fungi) A plantlike living thing that often gets its food from dead plants or animal material. Mushrooms and molds are both types of fungus.

genetic material The DNA in the nucleus (center) of a cell. Genes hold the information to build and maintain the cells that make up an animal or plant.

harpoon A weapon used for hunting large sea animals, especially whales. It consists of a barbed spear that is thrown by hand or fired from a gun.

larva (plural larvae) The young stage of an animal, usually an insect. The larva looks very different from the adult.

lemming A small, furry, short-tailed rodent found in the far north, close to the Arctic Circle.

mammal One of a group of warm-blooded animals that usually have fur or hair, and give birth to live young. Mammal mothers feed their young on milk produced from mammary glands. Humans, lions, and whales are all mammals.

marsupial A type of mammal that usually has a pouch where its young live for the early part of their lives. Kangaroos and opossums are marsupials.

mate An animal of the opposite sex, or to pair up with another animal of the opposite sex and reproduce.

metamorphosis A transformation or change in which the young form of an animal turns into a very different adult form.

migration When an animal makes a regular journey between two or more different places, often far apart to feed or to breed.

molt When an animal sheds its outer skin or covering.

nymph The young stage of an insect that undergoes partial metamorphosis.

offspring The young of an animal.

predator An animal that hunts and kills other animals for food.

pregnant Carrying developing offspring inside the body.

pupa A stage in the life cycle of some insects when the animal remains in one place, inside a protective casing, while its body changes from one form to another.

rainy season One of the two seasons that occur in tropical parts of the world (the other is the dry season).

reproduce To create offspring.

reptile One of a group of animals that are cold-blooded (cannot keep their body temperature constant), have a scaly skin, and lay leathery or hard eggs. Crocodiles, lizards and snakes are all reptiles.

sac A pouch made of thin skin or membrane.

scavenger An animal that eats the remains of dead animals and any other waste animal material.

sexual reproduction When a male cell joins a female cell (for example, when two animals mate) to produce offspring that inherit characteristics from both parents.

spawn To lay eggs (usually referring to fish, frogs, and toads), or the eggs laid by fish, frogs, and toads.

species One particular type of animal or plant. Members of the same species look similar and can breed together in the wild.

sponge A simple kind of animal that lives in water and feeds by extracting food from water that passes through the many holes in its body.

Further Information

Books

Animal Migration: Remarkable Journeys by Air, Land, and Sea by Ben Hoare (Natural History Museum, 2009)

Fusion: Life Processes and Living Things: Rotters! by John Townsend (Raintree, 2006)

The Life Cycle of Birds: From Egg to Adult by Mike Unwin (Heinemann Library, 2004)

The Life Cycle of Insects: From Egg to Adult by Louise Spilsbury (Heinemann Library, 2004)

Living Processes: Life Cycles by Richard Spilsbury (Rosen Central, 2010)

Websites

Animal Life Cycles and Dispersal (www.saburchill.com/ans02/chapters/chap044.html) *Learn more about why insects change from larvae to adults during their life cycle.*

Magicada Cicadas (www.magicicada.org/magicicada_straggler.php) *A mapping project about the amazing life cycle of cicadas.*

One Planet: Animal Migration in a Climate of Change (www.bbc.co.uk/programmes/w0006q63) *Listen to the story of monarch butterflies, wild geese, and other animal migrations.*

Pond Dipping with Gaby (www.rspb.org.uk/youth/play/dipping.asp) *Control Gaby's net to try and catch all the creatures in three different ponds.*

Index